D1737335

ANIMALS OF THE DESERT

Desert Tortoises

by Patrick Perish

BLASTOFF!
2
READERS

BELLWETHER MEDIA • MINNEAPOLIS, MN

Blastoff! Readers are carefully developed by literacy experts to build reading stamina and move students toward fluency by combining standards-based content with developmentally appropriate text.

Level 1 provides the most support through repetition of high-frequency words, light text, predictable sentence patterns, and strong visual support.

Level 2 offers early readers a bit more challenge through varied sentences, increased text load, and text-supportive special features.

Level 3 advances early-fluent readers toward fluency through increased text load, less reliance on photos, advancing concepts, longer sentences, and more complex special features.

★ **Blastoff! Universe**

Reading Level

Grade **K**

Grades **1–3**

Grade **4**

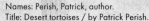

This edition first published in 2021 by Bellwether Media, Inc.

No part of this publication may be reproduced in whole or in part without written permission of the publisher. For information regarding permission, write to Bellwether Media, Inc., Attention: Permissions Department, 6012 Blue Circle Drive, Minnetonka, MN 55343.

Library of Congress Cataloging-in-Publication Data

Names: Perish, Patrick, author.
Title: Desert tortoises / by Patrick Perish.
Description: Minneapolis, MN : Bellwether Media, Inc., 2021. | Series: Blastoff! readers: animals of the desert | Includes bibliographical references and index. | Audience: Ages 5-8 | Audience: Grades K-1 | Summary: "Relevant images match informative text in this introduction to desert tortoises. Intended for students in kindergarten through third grade"-- Provided by publisher.
Identifiers: LCCN 2019054259 (print) | LCCN 2019054260 (ebook) | ISBN 9781644872208 (library binding) | ISBN 9781618919786 (ebook)
Subjects: LCSH: Desert tortoise--Juvenile literature.
Classification: LCC QL666.C584 P44 2021 (print) | LCC QL666.C584 (ebook) | DDC 597.92/4--dc23
LC record available at https://lccn.loc.gov/2019054259
LC ebook record available at https://lccn.loc.gov/2019054260

Editor: Rebecca Sabelko   Designer: Josh Brink

Printed in the United States of America, North Mankato, MN.

Table of Contents

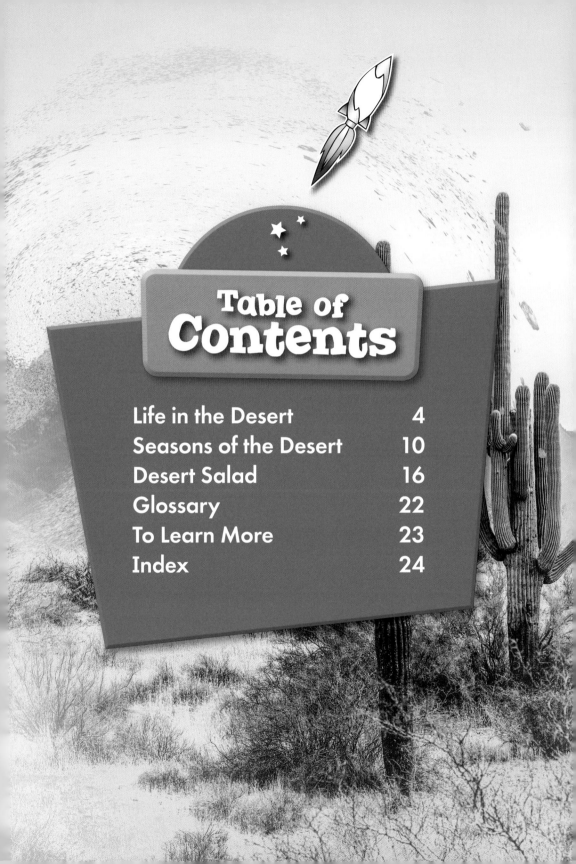

Life in the Desert

Desert tortoises are **reptiles**. They live in the southwestern United States and northwestern Mexico.

They are **adapted** to this dry desert **biome**.

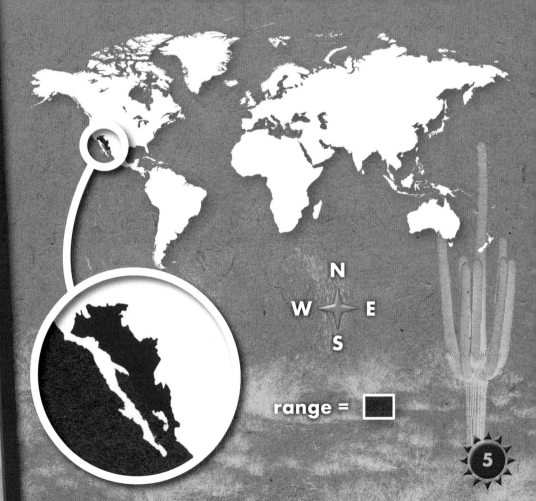

Desert Tortoise Range

N
W ✦ E
S

range = ▢

5

The desert is home to many **predators**. Hard shells keep these tortoises safe.

shell

scales

The desert ground is rough.
Scales on the front legs
keep the skin safe from cuts.

burrow

Desert tortoises have powerful front legs. They use their legs to dig **burrows** in the desert's dry ground.

8

Special Adaptations

scaly front legs

strong claws

hard shell

Their strong claws easily move rocks and sand.

Seasons of the Desert

Desert tortoises spend a lot of time in their burrows. They stay safe and cool on the hottest summer days.

10

They look for food when
it is not too hot outside.

These desert animals **hibernate** in winter. Their burrows do not get too hot or cold.

Five or more tortoises may share one burrow!

Spring and fall are busy
times in the desert! Plants
are fresh and green.

Desert tortoises spend
much of their days
searching for food.

Desert Salad

beak

Desert tortoises are **herbivores**. They eat grasses, wildflowers, and even cacti!

They use their beaks to tear tough desert plants.

Desert Tortoise Diet

desert
dandelions

prickly pear
cacti

white clovers

They dig small holes
in the ground to
catch water.

They hurry to get
a drink after **rare**
desert rains.

Desert Tortoise Stats

 Least Concern Near Threatened Vulnerable  Endangered Critically Endangered Extinct in the Wild Extinct

conservation status: vulnerable

life span: up to 80 years

Desert tortoises can go a long time without water. They store extra water in their bodies.

These amazing animals
are desert wonders!

Glossary

adapted—well suited due to changes over a long period of time

biome—a large area with certain plants, animals, and weather

burrows—holes or tunnels some animals dig for homes

herbivores—animals that only eat plants

hibernate—to spend the winter sleeping or resting

predators—animals that hunt other animals for food

rare—not common

reptiles—cold-blooded animals that have backbones and lay eggs

scales—small plates of skin that cover and protect a desert tortoise's body

To Learn More

AT THE LIBRARY

Atlantic, Leonard. *100-Year-Old Tortoises!* New York, N.Y.: Gareth Stevens Publishing, 2017.

Cocca, Lisa Colozza. *Desert Animals.* Vero Beach, Fla.: Rourke Educational Media, 2019.

Eboch, M.M. *Desert Biomes Around the World.* North Mankato, Minn.: Capstone Press, 2020.

ON THE WEB

FACTSURFER

Factsurfer.com gives you a safe, fun way to find more information.

1. Go to www.factsurfer.com.

2. Enter "desert tortoises" into the search box and click 🔍.

3. Select your book cover to see a list of related content.

Index

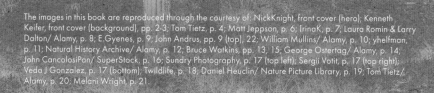